T0067182

Worthy Woman

I Am Worthy of All Things

Joshua
PHILLIPS

Edited by Samantha Graham

BALBOA.
PRESS

A DIVISION OF HAY HOUSE

Balboa Press books may be ordered through booksellers or by contacting:

Balboa Press
A Division of Hay House
1663 Liberty Drive
Bloomington, IN 47403
www.balboapress.com
1 (877) 407-4847

Because of the dynamic nature of the Internet, any web addresses or
links contained in this book may have changed since publication and
may no longer be valid. The views expressed in this work are solely those
of the author and do not necessarily reflect the views of the publisher,
and the publisher hereby disclaims any responsibility for them.

The author of this book does not dispense medical advice or prescribe the use
of any technique as a form of treatment for physical, emotional, or medical
problems without the advice of a physician, either directly or indirectly. The
intent of the author is only to offer information of a general nature to help
you in your quest for emotional and spiritual well-being. In the event you use
any of the information in this book for yourself, which is your constitutional
right, the author and the publisher assume no responsibility for your actions.

Any people depicted in stock imagery provided by Thinkstock are
models, and such images are being used for illustrative purposes only.
Certain stock imagery © Thinkstock.

Print information available on the last page.

ISBN: 978-1-5043-8131-4 (sc)
ISBN: 978-1-5043-8132-1 (e)

Balboa Press rev. date: 05/19/2017

The guide for every woman to enjoy the journey of having "IT" All!

Appreciations

I would like to first acknowledge several beautiful people in my life!

My mother Cynthia and my Grandmother Patsy for both being two strong women who raised me from birth. They have instilled determination, love, and sacrifice into me and I am grateful for their guidance.

My aunt Gerald, the woman who has always given me advice on life even when I didn't understand. She is a powerhouse and I am glad to be surrounded by your presence! Thank you!

My ex-step mom-now adopted "mom" Cheryl… the motivator in my life of many things… the love you give is out of this word.

To my extended family- Hannah, momma Shana, G-ma Stephanie, Kristyn, momma joy, Montana, Paris… Thank you all for your friendship and guidance and support.

To my sisters in arms, Elizabeth and Shardae. You are the definition of a powerhouse. You have been there every step of the way. You and I have shared over a decade worth of memories! From twirling in intermediate to marching in middle school to attending the same university, living together, churching together, and more. Thank you my "Sistas" for being there!

To my editor and high school best friend, Samantha Graham. Thank you for editing the entire book and giving me feedback on the journey! You are a powerhouse, go-getter, and I will forever love you! Thank you!

To my Mentors Blue, Dena and Margo, MITT Family and Coaches, and MSgt Judith Haskins. Thank you all for teaching me how to live in my truth and to be what the world needs!

Lastly, My love, Nicholas Jerome. I acknowledge you for building with me. For being the shoulder I can count on, person to laugh with, stay up all night with, count sit ups together with, Enjoy the exploration of food, and so many more things. You are an excellent example of what any man should be or want to become! Love you!

And to you Goddess, Thank you for investing into yourself and allowing me to take this powerful journey with you. This process is on your own time and I'm proud to lead you through it.

My Purpose

My intention for this book is to heal the heart, mind, and soul; to inspire you to live your life free and abundantly. To trust yourself and allow the universe to give you all that you desire. To live your purpose and allow love to be abundant in all areas of your life.

To allow yourself a new starting point that will allow you to redesign, build, and mold the life you have always dreamed of. To give you unconditional love and a supporting tool in life.

My purpose and passion is to allow yourself to see that you can have it all. You are a worthy Goddess, and that you, your dreams, and your purpose matter. You can have it all when you allow yourself to have it all!

My intention is for you to recognize fear and live your life anyway. To not allow fear to stop you and do anything and everything you always have or will want to do. YOUR purpose is a gift to the universe, and someone is waiting for you to step up and show out! You get to break free from your ego and comfort zone and allow yourself to create. Create magic, create greatness, create success, and love unconditionally!

My purpose is to build a community for women to be a part of so we can heal the world with love so we all can create our dreams and success.

My purpose is to extend the #MovementOfLove to you and your family!

Contents

When I own my power, who I truly am, I am in control of my life, Always!

Responsibility

Now ladies. This book isn't just another read for your book club, or a purchase to have on your coffee table, but an experiential journey into womanhood, feminine energy, and embracing all that is you! YES, YOU! There is nothing sexier, more giving, more gorgeous than seeing a Goddess (what I refer to women as) owning her own power, confidence, and strength. You are the creators of life, the givers of nature, the backbone for the masculine energy, as well as the providers of food and nurture.

Women have been the building blocks and foundation to healing this world. I am dedicated to treating every woman I come into contact with so they may use their feminine grace to improve the world we see.

Now responsibility is a topic to start off with for any individual. Are you responsible in all areas of your life? Are you holding others accountable? What does it mean to be responsible? Well, let's jump right in.

First, to be responsible means you are the author of your life. You have the pen and paper to create [or destroy] all within your life. To be responsible means you take action and acceptance of all things that have happened, will happen, and that you've created! You don't get to be a victim when life isn't going your way or when negative things happen. You get to take a look at how you, a woman, manifested those things. Did it start as a thought? Did you speak that particular action into the universe? Did you pray for something and this is just a lesson for that prayer to come to fruition? We have to be very conscious of our behavior, thoughts, and words because they do become actions.

Throughout the book, there will be different takeaways (nuggets) for you to use daily in your life to increase abundance in all things.

"When I come from a place of responsibility I own my power!"

What does that mean? We decide to stay neutral (not reacting positively or negatively) we have the control needed to get through all situations. When you are responsible, you allow yourself to create and take ownership. Being responsible could look like several things. Owning up to holding on to emotions that destroyed a friendship, apologizing for not allowing the world to see your gift, being a strong single mother that has raised all of your children alone, taking ownership of chasing your dreams, owning your own company, or allowing new creative connections to flow! Responsibility isn't a negative thing, it is allowing yourself to be in control of all things in your life.

But how can I be responsible if I didn't lie or cheat, and I did all I was supposed to? Well, great question. How can you? You can remember that everything that happens in life is for you and not against you. By living responsibly, you acknowledge your own strength. The universe, God, your higher power, always provides a lesson for you to learn, and in that lesson, you will gain personal growth! We will talk later about how things don't happen against you but for you!

Well, what about the pain? The pain is going to be there; you're human! You get to recognize the pain and sit with it for a bit then, by owning your strength you rise from the ashes, dust off the bruise, and jump right back in. I know, I know! Easier said than done right? RIGHT! You have to allow those conversations to take place in your head. If something is hard, it's because you make it that way, and the same principle applies to things that come with ease! YOU are in control of your own universe. Remember, we are staying in a responsible state of mind!

"When I say I can and I will-The universe provides a way."

So, ladies, you have homework! But this is fun and applies to everyday life.

Step one: Write down three things that have been bothering you for a long time, or that you have held on to.

Step two: Ask yourself, how can you come from a place of responsibility to change those situations?

Step three: Apply your action.

HERE'S an example for you to follow.

Step one: I don't talk to my mother (kids, brother sister cousin, whomever).

I didn't get the promotion at work because of (JANE OR JOE).

I don't like the way my body looks.

Step two: By being responsible,

I can forgive myself and allow the conversations to occur. I forgive myself for not talking to x, y, and z and I plan to connect with them right now. (Pick up the phone!!)

I did my best with the interview, and I know my worth. I didn't get the promotion this time but let me relax, redo, and retry. I got it the next time! This was a lesson to teach me about me! JANE OR JOE –I will congratulate them tomorrow in the office.

I have created this body, and I love it. It's not my best body, but I'm committed to changing it! I will start by walking three times a week on Monday Wednesday and Friday. I will also cut out red meat and drink at least 8 glasses of water every day. I love who I am, and I deserve to have the best body for me inside and out!

These are common problems that women experience. No person is the same or experiences the same situation so your answers could be the same and could be different.

When you do the work, you allow yourself the opportunity to grow.

My internal guide that leads me to the right roads in life... My intuition

Intuition

BOOM! BAM! I knew I was right!! I should have followed my first mind. I knew I had the correct idea. These are all common statements made by a human when we don't allow our "gut feeling" AKA your intuition to guide you. So what happened? Why didn't you follow your instinct? Why didn't you allow your intuition to guide you?

You have an internal compass that leads you and the decisions you make. A woman's intuition allows a woman to provide, to connect, to protect, to lead, to develop, and to excel. It is that "sixth sense" that allows freedom in many things. From dating to growing your business, to raising a child, to even building a family, your intuition is that inner feeling that pops up and says you're right or don't do that.

Now, let's not get that confused with your ego. Your ego is that voice inside your head that keeps you comfortable, safe if you will. Your intuition is that smart guy that allows you to be mindful of your situations. It provides you options and advice needed in a critical situation.

I've conducted several personal interviews with various women, and each has told me that their intuitions speak to them when they first meet people, or when put in a predicament to make a tough decision.

I believe your intuition is always present. Sometimes, we allow it to be pushed away or ignored because of our ego's stepping in and attempting to take over. Our ego is the reason many individuals second guess themselves.

> "THE ONLY REAL VALUABLE THING
> IS INTUITION."

> -Albert Einstein

Why is intuition so valuable? Why should you count on this "sixth sense"? What makes it so useful? You already have the answers to this. It's the internal guide that allows you to manifest all things with the direction of self. Mothers don't need to be trained to become a nurturing caregiver because of their intuitions. Women don't need to be taught how to be women because it is already a part of their intuition. Allow yourself to flow into the woman you are meant to become.

Homework:

Step one: Think back on three things where you originally had the right choice, and you decided not to go with that option. Journal why you decided not to go with your gut feeling. This journal should be a page in length. When you finish, move to step two.

Side note: Journaling is taking thoughts and writing them on paper. Journaling is freedom, release, creativity, and mediation. There are no rules on how to journal.

Step two: Get a note card and write this:

"I am a woman and my intuition is a gift to guide me. I have the choice to let it lead me in the right direction. This is my sixth sense, and I will own my intuition!"

Read it out loud to yourself for the next seven days!

When I take care of myself, I have much to give from a full bucket!

Self-Care

To define the word care, we must first understand self. We get to take a hard look at ourselves inside and out before we apply care. To start off this chapter, we will do something important. IMAGE! How many women dislike their body? From the way they look naked to the extra belly fat, or loose skin around the arms or even the stubborn hair that grows in all the wrong places. From waxing to shaving, there are multiple ways to hide behind an image we create! So the most important thing is to first recognize and acknowledge self!

ACTIVITY:

Step one: Get a blank sheet of paper and draw yourself. You don't need it to be artistic and look like a Mona Lisa painting. IT CAN BE STICK FIGURES! But make sure you enjoy the process of drawing yourself. When you draw yourself, go into a private place like your bathroom, remove all of your clothing and stand in the mirror. Set a timer and look at yourself for a minute in silence. Don't say anything and allow your mind to be free and just look. Things may come up for you. Things such as happiness, sadness, fear, accomplishment, defeat and other emotions.

Feel each emotion as they come. Once the minute has passed then get your paper and draw the body you saw in the mirror, not the body you want or would like.

Step two: For every part of your body you dislike draw a little heart over it. Remember we are changing the conversations we have with ourselves so no, I MEAN NO, negative thoughts. The hearts represent things you want to love on extra now. So, if you don't like the extra roll on your stomach now's your chance to take the time to love on it. That means changing the conversation in your head from I'm fat into "I GET TO HAVE MY BEST BODY!" After you show yourself where to send a little extra love, this will help you prepare for self-care. Usually, the way we feel on the inside is reflected externally.

Care starts with you! Ladies, this means for self-care it's all about YOU! When we apply self-care, you temporarily resign from all positions such as mom, wife, sister, girlfriend, aunt, boss best helper, a slave at work, errand girl for neighbor and family members, and anything else you are committed to! This is where balance plays a great role. Life isn't going to stop because of self-care, but you can say Universe it's time for me!

So what exactly is self-care? As Jenna Phillips Ballard would say, "you get to be a unicorn." You get to do all things that make you feel good inside and out. This could be getting your nails and toes done at the nail shop, a day trip to your favorite spot, taking yourself to lunch or dinner and enjoying a nice glass of wine, watching a movie at the movie theater, having a day out with girlfriends, shopping, or exploring a new place. Any activity that you enjoy doing alone or with others. When you take care of yourself you are telling the universe, "I MATTER" and "I receive this." You are also saying that you will allow others to care for you and attract the things into your life that will support this! This could mean attracting the man of your dreams if you're single or going back to the day you met your spouse. Whatever it may be you deserve this Goddess.

Think about a bucket filled to the rim with money. If the bucket is overflowing with money, you will have enough to give away. If the bucket is empty, you will have nothing to give away. Caring for yourself is the same. If you are burnt out, not fueled, depleted, you will have nothing to give back to your life, relationships, job or career, or anything that surrounds you! You must make sure the inside is taking care of, and the outside will follow.

A lot of the times you forgot about yourself as women or even as a person. You put the title's you carry before taking care of yourself. NO NO NO NO MA'AM! Not anymore! Say "I COME FIRST."

A Powerful way to receive is simply to declare!

Affirmations

An affirmation is like a universal declaration. It is you telling the universe who and what you are, so in return that is what comes your way. When you create an affirmation you are stating something as a fact. You can have positive affirmations or negative ones.

Let's take a look at you! Do you feel happy? Do you have all the money you wish you had? Do you have the man or woman of your dreams? Do you have the job you have always wanted? Do you have the car you've dreamed of since middle school? Do you have the marriage or house you want? Have you traveled to all the places you want? Etc.

After you start questioning your life, you will realize you have sold yourself short! You have been playing small in the world but that's okay. You can change how you play this game called "LIFE." But how do you do this? Simple! Positive affirmations and committed actions. Well, what is a positive affirmation?

I WILL HAVE An excellent day!

I WILL CREATE JOY AND LAUGHTER!

I WILL LOVE UNCONDITIONALLY!

I AM courageous. I AM Beautiful. I AM whole.

Before we can make or write out our affirmations, we should pay attention to the story we are telling ourselves. Below are some examples of stories you may tell yourself and then how you can create a positive Declaration (affirmation).

Career/job

The story you might tell yourself: I HATE working. I have the worst coworkers. I hate my boss. This isn't the career you want to be in so:

Positive Declaration: I am thankful for this Job (career). I am creating the space so others may fill this position. OR I am calling for an electrifying career where I am being compensated for my worth.

Money/Finances

The story you may tell yourself: I will always be broke. My account is always in the negative. I don't make a lot of money. I am going to be poor. Forever broke!

Positive Declaration: I am financially abundant. I appreciate all funds I have in my wallet and my bank account. I have all the money I need for all the things I want to do. I am financially free. I am free from a broke mentality. I am always abundant.

Something I have personally suffered from is always thinking the world was out to get me. I thought everything that was happening to me was personally against me. From this, I learned the next positive declaration of letting go and understanding not to take every situation personally.

The story you may tell yourself: They are attacking me. People are mad at me because of X Y Z. If you have this type of conversation and have taken anything personal, this is a declaration that will help you.

Positive Declaration: I am in control of my life so no one can take my power away. It is okay just to listen because this isn't about me. It's okay to let go!

How did you feel reading the stories you tell yourself? Angry. Sad. Depressed. Emotional. Irritated. Bothered. Incomplete. Small. Belittled. Taken advantage of. No power. No purpose. Etc. BUT the game changer is when we change those stories into positive declarations. It makes us feel empowered.

Go-getters. Positive. Worthy. Incredible. Big. Important. Making a difference in our lives. Great. Impactful.

Goddesses!

When you change your stories, you modify the outcome. When you speak positively, you attract positivity!

I am the creator of all that happens to me, for me, and through me!

Things Happen For You
Not Against You

T hings happen for you, not against you. Accept that as truth!

This chapter's dedicated to the internal feeling or the internal question to do something. When you have to ask should I or shouldn't I... this is the chapter to read!

Have you ever felt an internal calling for something? Like making a drastic change in your life. Things like: leaving a long term relationship, changing a career after eight years, or just moving to a different state or part of the world on an instant thought. We all have an ability to be connected to the universe, and our passions inspire us from within. Think about your favorite thing to do and pay attention to how you feel when doing that activity or hobby. It is like a euphoric feeling that sometimes can't be described. It's a condition that you would love to have all the time. It's the imagery of being on cloud nine every day. Right! This inner feeling is what I have deemed the "internal calling." Internally your body is persuading you to accept that call and pursue it. Your ego and comfort zone will tell you all the reasons you shouldn't but deep down you know you want to! This is the answer for you to do it! You no longer have to question if it's right for you? Is it the right timing? Should I wait? Etc. My response to all of that is why wait? Why put off another dream for another time. Why not live free and do what your heart desires? So I say: YES to leaving that toxic relationship. YES to following your passion and leaving the exhausting slave job you have. YES to ending friendships because they don't align with who you are and where you are going. YES to allowing yourself to be happy with any and all decisions. YES to being an independent, beautiful, powerful goddess who walks in her truth daily. YES to sharing your stories with everyone so anyone can get who you are! YES to owning your power and saying no! Saying no is simply a gift to all. Saying no allows you to stand in your power and the gift of allowing someone else to stand in theirs. Saying no is an opportunity for someone to say yes!

This is the answer you have been looking for. This is your YES! This is the yes that will be the most powerful yes you have ever said. Take a moment and stand in front of the mirror for a minute without saying anything. After your minute, as loudly as you possibly can shout YES! YES TO ME! YES TO Me! YES TO WHATEVER YOU WANT TO GIVE A YES TO! This moment may be the first time in a while that you allow yourself to feel whole, complete, and in your power!

Sometimes, we get so caught up in allowing our lives to become autopilot. Wake up, eat, drive to work, eat lunch, work some more, drive home, get the kids or pick up dinner, eat, repeat every day for the rest of your life. How does it feel to be in a routine of something that doesn't excite you? How does it feel to be working and living someone else's dreams and not your own? How does it feel to have the greatest ideas idle in your head instead of sharing them with the world? The only person you have to fight is yourself. If you are saying YES to all that you are then you are allowing yourself to manifest all your dreams! If money didn't exist and If you could do anything in the world, live anywhere in the world, or vacation at any place in the world, where would you go, what you would you do, who do you see yourself with? NOW make that reality. Don't allow your comfort zone and ego to keep you in a box of limited opportunity when the world is waiting for you to share your gift.

THIS IS YOUR ANSWER! THIS IS YOUR YES!

Pain To Passion (Healing The Hurt And Sharing Your Story)

LADIES... LADIES... LADIES! Have you ever been hurt? Have you ever felt a broken heart? Are you in pain now? Not just physical pain, but emotional pain, psychological pain, mental pain, or even spiritual pain. I am sure some of you are, and even if not right in this moment, you have experienced enough of it in your life.

RAPE. MOLESTATION. ABUSED. BEATEN. HIT ON. BODY SHAMED. BELITTLED.

CHEATED ON. CHEATER. SEX ENTHUSIAST. PROSTITUTION. PRETTY. UGLY. FAT. SKINNY. ROLLS. CURLY HAIR. STRAIGHT HAIR. TOO DARK.

Whatever the story may be, it is you! Do you know how many girls and women in the world are going through, right now, what you have already been through? Do you know that someone just committed suicide because they thought they were alone? Do you know you are powerful beyond measure and your message can save lives?

The shit you went through as a little girl, a young lady, and now a woman gets to be heard. Change the story in your mind and allow yourself to be vulnerable. Change the pressure of fear to passion without pain. Change your PAIN into PASSION.

What does this mean? It means you get to heal from said story. Let go of feelings that may have lingered from the past, heal, and allow yourself to share your story. Someone out there is waiting for you to share it. So how do you heal? How do you let go? How do you stop being afraid and live freely? First, acknowledge yourself for being strong enough to have experienced that "horrible story." Not everyone makes it, but you did! You have a purpose, and that experience has made you ready for anything and everything in life. You have been granted the gift of gratitude because you went through that crap alone and now you get to inspire others. So here are a few helpful tools for acknowledgment, healing, and turning that pain into PASSION!

To acknowledge yourself, stand in front of a mirror or anything that allows you to see yourself clearly. Stare yourself in the eyes for about two to three minutes. Allow your mind to roam and be free for those two to three minutes. If you feel negative thoughts coming up, allow them but focus on the positive. If you get stuck with not having one positive thing to say use this one. "I am alive and can create whatever I want to today!" After the few minutes have passed, say aloud, "I acknowledge (your name) for...

Some things that you can acknowledge is: being brave, beautiful, giving, caring, nurturing, kind hearted, or loving. OR you could acknowledge yourself for things you have done or currently do such as: sharing knowledge, empowering others, mentoring others, learning, teaching, working, supporting others, raising children or a child, long lasting relationships, friendships, etc.

So how does it feel to be acknowledged by yourself? What I have gathered and from personal experiences is that I felt rewarded, great, interested, loved, cared for, and appreciated. There is no limit on the number of things you can acknowledge yourself for but do it until you smile on the inside.

If you want to take it a step further, recognize other people in your life. All you have to do is pick up the phone or meet for lunch and just let them know how you feel about them and what you appreciate them for. Trust me, they may think something is weird, or you want something from them but it's all from a genuine place. When was the last time you told someone I love you just because… I'm grateful for you because… I love your… Etc.

Next, write down this pain that you have or have held on to for so long. It is time to let it go! The only way you can change your PAIN into your PASSION is by acknowledging it, accepting it, healing it, and sharing it.

Next, accept that it has happened for you and not to you! Sometimes, we tell ourselves certain things based on a specific event. For example, I am not good enough because I failed at XYZ. This is called a story. If you change the story you've created you then can change the results. It is all about perspective now. Accepting it is just allowing yourself to feel how you feel, and making the decision to say this has happened but from this day forward I am not letting it hurt me anymore. I am free from that experience. It has been with me for all this time, and I am finally letting it go! Accepting it can be really just that simple so try not to complicate it. Accepting it may involve you talking to a close friend or family member.

Which leads us to the healing phases! How do you heal something that felt like it destroyed you? Address it head on! This is something you do for yourself and not for others. So approach the pain with confidence and as a free woman! This could be achieved multiple ways. For example, phone call, meeting for lunch or dinner, writing a letter to a person, writing a letter and burning it (symbol of releasing), punching a punching bag, painting, screaming until you have released all of the built up emotions out, crying your heart out, writing, etc. Discover your own healing process for your pain. This is just a guide to it.

Lastly, sharing it! No, you are not going to share your pain with someone, but you will share the success story that was created from your pain. This is you being in service and allowing someone to hear you, see you, trust you, find you, open up to you, or even be inspired by you. Sharing your story will allow others to see you inside and out and enable them to connect with you on a different and much deeper level. Your story will change someone's life so don't hold out. Share how you find yourself in a horrible marriage. Share how you were raped and now mentor people who are survivors of rape. Share how someone close to you was killed by a drunk driver and that was your motivation to create organizations to stop drunk driving. Share how you want to build nonprofits for girls because as a girl growing up you didn't have a mom or dad and you want them to know they have someone! Share your Pain and make it a passion.

So with transparency and vulnerability, I changed my pain into passion.

As a young boy, I was raped. At the time, I didn't realize it was rape. Years went by because I thought it was normal for an older man to want to have sex with me. The thing is young boys do grow up. I called it experimenting. I just knew this was a way of life, but what I didn't understand is why I had to hide to do it or why I couldn't say anything to anyone. But I never said a peep because I knew I would not get to experiment anymore. When I got older and understood what rape was, it devastated me. I felt like I was dirty and didn't deserve to be on this earth anymore. I got extremely depressed and instead of letting someone know I held on to that pain. I held on to it so much that I wanted my body to be numb. Every day I would cut myself in places people couldn't see. My intention was to cut myself until one day I bled to death. One day, I stopped the cutting and substituted something else. I would sleep with men, use them, and then never speak to them again. Think of a black widow spider. Once she was done with the male spider, she would kill them. I was the human version of the black widow. I didn't kill them, but I would cause unnecessary pain towards them. I didn't even care if I would get hurt because I got to hurt them. Do you see how dangerous that mentality can be? There are many people with similar stories out there.

Well, the feeling to go numb never really went away until I started my healing process. Ladies, I held on to this pain for years before I decided I wanted something better for myself. So I began acknowledging myself. Telling and showing myself that I am not dirty, but a loving caring and powerful man. That I belong on this earth to inspire a global change. That I am better than my situations, and they don't define me. I began acknowledging what I have done in school, the community, careers, and for anyone. This was just the beginning. I then accepted the truth that I am a survivor of rape! DAMN! That is powerful! Just like your acceptance will be. I SURVIVED! That showed me strength. And then the healing. I couldn't heal the scars that I had held onto for so long by myself, so first it was counselors. Then it went to a psychologist. Then it went to me going to church and speaking with the pastor. Then it went to venting to friends, Facebook, and fuck buddies. Then I just sat in my room and cried because none of that was working. I didn't feel any healing going on. So I gave up and held onto it for some time longer. Then I was introduced to emotional intelligence and BAM those four months of training taught me about my mind and how powerful it is! I wasn't healing because I didn't want to heal. I wanted to be a victim of my story so others could feel sorry for me. It was a twisted idea and honestly I was hurting myself. After I had taken multiple courses, talked to a couple of life coaches and spiritual leaders, I began addressing my pain full force. Ladies, some things you just will not be able to do on your own. Ask for support. Ask for guidance. AND THEN I finally change my pain into my passion! As someone who felt that my childhood was taken away and that I literally wanted to die when I was a child, I decided to do the necessary work to ensure no child feels this way. A MOVEMENT was created. MY MOVEMENT. A MOVEMENT OF LOVE! I decided to become an empowerment warrior to heal the hearts, mind, and souls of any and all individuals I come in contact with. I have started my own business as a life coach, speaker, and empowerment enthusiast to ensure childhoods are valued. In between my pain and passion, I discovered women I get to work with and heal as well so this is one of the many things I am doing for women. This book is for any woman who has experienced hurt or pain at any time in their life and how you get to stand in your truth! So this is me sharing my pain and turning it into passion.

Now it's your turn to share your pain and show your passions. Even if you don't know what your passion is yet, share your story so it can reach someone else and potentially save their life. When you do share it hashtag #MovementOfLove.

—ɯ—

Confidence: Shine Your Feminine Grace

C lick. Clack. Click. Clack. Click is the sound a heel makes when a woman drives her foot into the ground. Her dress is well fitted, feeling sexy as ever, and having the time of your life. Do you remember a day like this? Do you remember that one time you got all dressed up in makeup, hair, clothes, clutch, shoes and accessories to match and felt absolutely beautiful and confident? Where did she go? Do you need all the extras to feel confident and beautiful inside and out? The answer is HELL NO!

Ladies, your confidence is sexy! To be able to love all that is you brings a glow, a shine to you that radiates to everyone. To be in your "feminine grace" allows your inner beauty to shine and be on showcase for the world. The question is, are you ready for that? Are you prepared to walk in your truth and allow the world to see how beautiful you really are!

First, you must be okay with all that is you! LOVE that extra roll that you have. Love that extra fat underneath your arm that you want to get rid of. Love the extra weight you put on the last six months. Love those ex-lovers who broke your heart and have made you strong. Girlfriends, Love all that is you because it is beautiful! The outer beauty is not what should be seen first, but the inner beauty is what should radiate. So what does it mean to allow your confidence to be seen or to let your feminine grace shine?

It means owning your power and strength. Being confident is allowing yourself to be free and make your own rules. In this game of life, you have the ability to manifest whatever you desire, and that is powerful. So instead of worrying about what Ronda, Janet, or Tim thinks about you, instead concentrate on what you know about you. Let us take a look at a few things that may be affecting you from truly owning your confidence.

So you think you are fat or unattractive:

Well, you are not! You are beautiful, and you get to own everything you dislike. So, if it is an unwanted dimple, extra roll, excess skin, pimple, love handles, weird shaped toe, an extra finger, two noses, etc. you get to own it.

> "WHEN I OWN AND DISPLAY MY FLAWS I ALLOW BEAUTY TO EXIST."
>
> - Joshua Phillips

Now ladies, when I say you get to own it I mean you get to be okay with your differences and create a healthy and happy way to get to what you desire. If you are 180 pounds and want to get back to 150 pounds all you have to do is love yourself, love the food you put in your body, love that weekly exercise routine, and love your journey of weight loss. If you don't feel great about doing it by yourself, invest in a friend or personal trainer and allow them to coach you through it.

"OUR FLAWS IS WHAT MAKES US UNIQUE AND BEAUTIFUL."

-Joshua Phillips

Say you don't like your skin color because it is splashy or uneven and you use makeup to cover it up.

STOP! Someone in the world besides you is looking for his/her queen with an uneven tone of skin.

BABY, you get to own it because it is beautiful.

Say you don't like the love handles you have. Well, let's be honest, some men love women who have a little extra that he can grab onto! From holding you tight at night to making love to you, or even just to tickle you. He wants to love you, and you get to love yourself. Everything is not about a spouse, but the things you are running from are some of the qualities that attract people to you.

Do you have that one person in your life or celebrity that you like, and you always say she is gorgeous or she is beautiful? You get to realize that she owns her feminine grace just like you will start doing after this chapter! There is no difference between you and them!

But I don't feel comfortable doing that or wearing something like that or allowing him to do that? How about you try it and see what happens. If you don't like it cool, but at least try it a few times before you say it is not for you.

Let us discuss a few things you can do to start leveling up your confidence/Feminine grace meter.

First, acknowledge all the things you love about your body. Then all the things that you would like to enhance. Now look in the mirror and tell yourself that even though you don't have your best (fill in the blank or blanks), it is okay because today is the first day of my life that I am okay with what I have.

Example: Josh, even though I don't have a six-pack, small feet, even arms, darker skin, or a hairless body, today is the first day of my life that I am okay with not having those things. Today is the first day of the rest of my life that I get to work towards my best body! Whatever it is that you want to work towards tell yourself that. Be honest with yourself and watch how this little saying will slowly start to change your life. Write it down and say it every morning before starting your regular routine.

Next, gather a few girlfriends and do some self-care together. Own your feminine grace and be girly for a day or every day. Go to the nail shop or stay in and paint them yourself, get your teeth whitened, go thrift shopping, go to the movies, have a girl's night with some wine and relaxation or just sleep in, but whatever you decide to do, allow yourself to just take care of you and not everyone else.

The last thing you get to do when focusing on your feminine grace is to not care what others think of you! The Debbie Downer and Negative Nancy doesn't matter! You will have those type of people all your life but don't allow them to dim your light. If you have felt you have been different your entire life, then continue to be different. If someone told you that you may be a little weird then be a lot of weird. OWN THAT SHIT! Allow yourself to be free and do what you love, wear what you love, invest into what you love, and share what you love! I guarantee that when you stop allowing yourself to give two dimes about others and start focusing on yourself, your life will start to feel amazing.

JUST BE YOU! And if someone doesn't like it they can just suck your big toe!

The Energy... Masculine And Feminine

G O GO GO nonstop can be exhausting. When you look at you current situations, and you take a look at how manly the things you are doing are, that my friend, is the masculine energy. When you are always chasing, controlling, being in charge of everything, and hunting you are suppressing your feminine energy and only allowing the masculine energy to work. Do you know why this is so harmful to you as a woman?

There are many reasons. First, you are going against your natural state. You as a woman are made to receive. Let us connect this to relationships. If you are a single woman and wishing for a partner to come into your life but you are trying to control everything, it is not going to happen! If you emasculate a man and don't allow him to be a man, then you aren't going to be happy in a relationship because you aren't attracting what you need or want. If you are a powerhouse in your career and at the top of your leadership chain but don't make time for yourself, friends, hobbies, social activities, or your partner you are in your masculine energy.

So being in your masculine energy and feminine energy is a balance for women and men. So how do we create the balance? You must first learn your masculine traits and your feminine traits. Below is a list of things that could be considered masculine and/or feminine. Masculine:

Expression of power
Take ownership
Accomplishing
Self-confidence
Focused
Promptness
Aggressive

Feminine:

Expression of love
Worthy of others
Doing what is right
Giving
Selfless
Compassion
Kindness
Caring

As you can tell, multiple traits can be considered in your masculine or feminine. In life, you don't get to be just masculine or feminine. It is an interchange and balance of the energies. You may be in your masculine, a go-getter, results oriented, deadlines now, at work but when you get home, you may be in your feminine.

When we look at masculinity and femininity, it's not looking at woman or man but the energy you are working in. Everything doesn't require immediate action, aggressiveness or a loud tone. Instead, you may need just to receive, relax and manifest.

Men are typically about 60-70% in the masculine energy and women are 60-70% in the feminine energy, but there is a balance between both. A healthy relationship with work, school, friends, family, relationships, and partnerships all require different energies at different times.

Recognize where you are in all areas of life and see how you can balance it. Better results are yet to come!

Fear

re you currently doing what you have always wanted? Are you living in the location you dreamed of, working your dream job, or traveling the world? Maybe. Maybe not. But why ladies? Why don't you have all that you have ever wanted or desired?

Hmm. Money? Ambition? Friends? People telling you no? People saying you will never be able to do that? Stories you have made up in your head? Limiting beliefs about self? OR simply fear? Fear of the unknown? Fear of what could or could not happen? Fear of actually being successful? Or fear of just how the world will receive your Awesomeness?

All roads lead back to fear.

"Stop being captain save a hoe and save yourself!"

Whether you realize it now or later, fear is always present in our lives. It never goes away. What could be stopping you from having all you desire is operating out of fear, displacing it, or putting things on the back burner because of it. Instead of doing those things, you get to walk directly into what has you fearful. What would it look like if you just said, "YES! This scares the hell out of me, but I am going for it anyway!" Don't you think life would be so much more meaningful to you if you enjoyed every area of it?

I don't have the money. I don't have the time. I don't have the energy. And guess what? You are settling into your current situations and allowing that to control your life and freedom. If you continue to allow the things you currently don't have to stop you, then you will never be happy one hundred percent. Fear can be minute, or it can be a significant component of your life, but we will discuss how you can change your fears into figures ☺

First, eliminate the conversation of you can't! Being fearful and in your comfort zone doesn't allow you to live freely. Being in your comfort zone or allowing your fear to control you will only enable you to be miserable or just "content." What if you said, "I can and I will?" The universe may send you some minor challenges and bumps on your journey to greatness, but it isn't going to stop you! You stop yourself when you say, "I can't." The only person that ever stops you from living abundantly is you!

For example, "I can't quit my job because I don't have savings put away, I don't have another job yet, or the support, etc. First, read the chapter on affirmations, then create a positive affirmation regarding the things you say you can't complete. So, after that positive affirmation and mentally saying you can, I guarantee things will start unfolding for you. You get to realize how fear affects you! You'll have the ability to stare at your fear and still accomplish your goals. Fear never goes away, but you can walk directly into it and own it! So this job you want to quit, if you can't do it today create a four-week to do list and put it into the universe. The time frame can change based on where you are in life and what you want to accomplish but realize LIFE is now! Don't plan a six-month journey when you can commit yourself to a balls to the wall, do whatever it takes, three-month plan.

That relationship or marriage that isn't going anywhere get out of it! You don't have to continue to sacrifice your happiness and well-being to be in partnership with someone. Girl let him or her go! "IT ISN'T WORTH IT!" Drop them off where you found them and allow yourself to be who you are! Being your authentic, genuine, loving self, allows for your partner to encounter you and court you! You don't need that toxic relationship. Today is the last day you will be in any toxic relationships!

So you want to travel the world but can't because of money? Well, if you continue to focus on money and how it is stopping you, then you will forever not have what you want! Change your conversation and leave money/ finances out of it. Focus on what you want to do and what you are good at doing. Allow what you offer to be your income, and the universe will provide for you. Committed action and lowering fear will get you to your goal. When you are abundant in all things, the universe allows for all things to come to you! Find your passion and make that into business for yourself. Someone is waiting on that idea you have that you haven't acted on yet.

We can discuss all things in life that are stopping us but take a moment and do some goal planning. What do you want to accomplish in the next year? After you write out your goals, how can you achieve them in six months? Stop procrastinating on your life, your freedom, and your dreams. Let's get to it now and allow your best self to be present. Today is the last day that you will allow fear to stop you!

Below are a few exercises to help you get started and jumping right into fear!

Singers: ask to sing in the office, on a plane while boarding, in the mall, or whatever. Just do it for the crowd and listen to the reactions.

Dancers: dance anywhere and everywhere.

Workaholics: Take a day or two off work and do some self-care! Shut off all phones and laptops and allow the business to run itself and you invest into yourself! I promise you it will be there when you return.

People not living your purpose: OKAY! This is the last time I will tell you to follow your heart! DO IT NOW! Stop investing in other people's dreams and invest in your own. It is time for you to have all you desire. Don't worry about family, friends, money, cars, or shelter simply worry about getting your dream up and running.

People who want to travel: Go alone or with a group. Plan your first trip for within the next three months. DO IT NOW! A whole new country or state wants you there!

People who want to move: just do it already! Stop worrying about the "what if's" and just go. Pack up all of your things and get to that new destination. If you have nothing there, use that as a fire to get everything you want when you arrive.

Ladies, whatever it is you want to accomplish do it now. Fear can be in the form of people saying don't do it; you can't do it, or I don't think you should do it. Thank them for sharing and follow your heart! "This is for me to grow and it is what is best for me."

ARE YOU READY TO LIVE AND LET FEAR GO?

Giving (Stop Doing It For Everyone Else And Do It For Yourself).

E xhausted. Drained. Empty. Tired. Restless. Irritated. Annoyed. Depleted.

Imagine a bucket that is used to carry water for drinking. That bucket has an important purpose. If you have no bucket, then you can't transport water to wherever it is needed. So you gather the bucket, get to some form of a water source, and now you are carrying it back to where you need it. Say for instance the water is for drinking and cooking purposes. You get home and pour some in a pot and some in a cup. The cup of drinking water is used to nourish your body and the water in the pot is used to cook with, which eventually will produce something to fuel and nourish your body. Do you see the importance of not only the water but the bucket as well?

So imagine you are the bucket and all the great things you have is the water. Your water could be happiness, money, gratitude, love, freedom, nourishment, food, light, etc. If your bucket (your body) is depleting of those things, how could you possibly give it away? Is it starting to make more sense? We are only able to give what we have in abundance. If the bucket is overflowing then there is plenty to give, but if the bucket is empty then there is nothing to give.

"When I give abundantly I receive abundantly."

How often are you giving to all those around you and not replenishing or giving to yourself? Maybe you are not sleeping a full eight hours a night but working fifty plus hours a week. Perhaps you are running a marathon of errands but haven't stopped for a balanced, healthy meal at all. How do you run off of no energy? How do you continually deplete your stock of awesomeness for others? HMM…

Well, there is a great answer and fix for this incredible challenge. You get to be you and acknowledge when it is time to focus on self, so there is enough to give externally. Focusing on yourself will be interesting for you as you dive deep into what you already have! Ladies a big one is love! Love yourself first and then love all that's around you. I know it is sometimes hard to love everything you are before loving those around you, but it makes everyone stronger. If you allow people to see how awesome it is to love yourself, you will naturally create a domino effect of people wanting to enjoy themselves. The person who benefits the most from self-love is you and the people around you! Your husband or wife, kids, work/career, siblings, friends or family are not an excuse for you to use to deplete all that you have. As elders have always told us, "Invest into yourself first and all will come!"

So refer to the water and bucket and compare it to all that's in your life. Remember, you are the bucket and that bucket gets to overflow in all areas of your life.

Always give, be loving, and be abundant! You get to have it all and give it all, but the most important first step is self-care!

When you begin to give and keep your bucket overflowing, let someone know and share the message. We don't have to kill ourselves to give to others. So let's #GivingWithoutDestruction!

Receiving

T ake a deep breath, inhale for four seconds, hold for four seconds and exhale for four seconds.

Again. Take a deep breath in for four seconds, hold for four seconds and exhale for four seconds. Two more times, take a deep breathe in for four seconds, hold for four seconds and exhale for four seconds. Last time, take a deep breathe in for four seconds, hold for four seconds and exhale for four seconds.

Imagine the air you just breathed in was filled with everything you needed for the rest of your life. The universe created that special air for you to inhale. Let's just think about how valuable that air is to us. Somewhere in the world, a plant seed was planted. It grew big and vigorous. One of its many purposes was to clean the dirty carbon dioxide and release precious oxygen. That precious oxygen was just inhaled by you. Now realize for the plant to grow it needed water and sunlight, the ground, and love. It was given all those things, and now it cleans the air for us allowing breathable air. Have you ever just appreciated the flow and process of the air we breathe? Probably not. And that's okay. Receiving can be just like inhaling air.

As a woman, you are naturally made to receive in your life. Biologically configured, it is who the universe created you to be. But do you allow yourself to receive or are you always trying to be in your masculine and chase or hunt things?

You have the ability to call into your life what you want and desire. All you have to do is be open to receiving. It is okay to allow the universe to give you things because rightfully you probably have done something beforehand to receive such a great gift. Receiving love from your partner or new lover is okay. It is okay to receive money when someone is offering it to you. It is okay to receive support when you can't finish something by yourself. It is okay to receive feedback from those in your life, It allows growth. It is okay to receive confirmations of what you are doing is the path you should be on. LADIES, IT IS OKAY!

You don't always have to be the go getter, the breadwinner, the queen bitch, the one who sacrifices, the commander, the rug who gets walked on, or just a parent. You get to receive all that you are and more and allow yourself to be great in the world! But how?

Well, there is a process, and I would start with breathing and connecting each breath to something in your life. Every time you take a breath, be very conscious of what your thoughts are while inhaling and exhaling. You get to inhale nothing but positive vibes while only exhaling negative vibes or things that don't serve you in life. So inhale things like good health, abundance, freedom, nourishment, and good energy. Exhale things like: negative vibes, depression, abuse, negative emotions, and anything you want to let go.

This process allows you to connect to the universe and become grounded in your life. It lets you focus on what you are calling into your life and the things you get to let go of or move forward from. It is a process designed to get you centered and aligned! Deep breathing is a form of meditation and allows you to calm. The great thing about deep breathing is that you can do it throughout the day and for a few minutes. Receiving isn't hard until we make it hard and attach stories we have created. It is time for you to let those stories go and be free... you are a Goddess, and get to receive all that is in life for you.

Things you are worthy of receiving:

Receive that man/woman you have asked for.

Receive that career you have always wanted.

Receive that promotion at work.

Receive that vacation paid for by someone else.

Receive the thank you that you get a great job or just being awesome.

Receive that free babysitter just because.

Receive the gifts you receive and don't ask why.

Receive yourself for being freaking awesome.

Receive your blessings from the universe.

Receive the compliment that came out of nowhere.

Receive the person who always flirts with you.

Receive the paid purchase that you will experience at checkout.

Receive the whole can of soda a Flight attendant may give you on the plane.

Receive the incredible scenery or view at home or while on vacation.

Receive paradise into your life wherever you are.

Receive love from all those in your life.

Receive change as it allows you to grow.

Receive guidance as it allows change.

Receive your own intuition as it leads you to greatness.

Receive your Goddess as it is your strength.
Receive your purpose as it is your destiny.
Receive all things because you are WORTHY of receiving!

It's okay to Receive, you are worthy!

—ᴍ—

Gratitude

Thankfulness. Appreciation. Gratefulness. Appreciativeness.
Acknowledgement. Recognition. Respectfulness.

Do you ever have a euphoric feeling when you appreciate the things you already have? Sometimes in life, we get so buckled down in chasing our dreams and forget to enjoy the process or the journey we are on. We forget to acknowledge our growth over periods of time. Well, Goddess, this is your slight pause to allow yourself just to be recognized and simply be grateful for what you have already. I acknowledge you for reading this book to enhance everything in your life. I acknowledge you for being a strong woman and surviving all that's been thrown at you over the years. I acknowledge you for saying enough is enough and taking on the first day of the rest of your life. I acknowledge you for being a big ball of awesomeness. I acknowledge you for being you and learning who you are! I acknowledge you for the pain, hurt, sweat and tears throughout life that you've experienced. I acknowledge you for your #HerStory. Your "HerStory" is the same as History. I acknowledge you for being the rope needed and used to keep families together, friends together, relationships together and your dreams together. I acknowledge you for giving so much and not wanting anything in return. When you give you know it is for a good cause and you know it will come back some way. I acknowledge you for your strength; it is not easy being a woman in a world where many don't appreciate you! I acknowledge you Goddess! You are so much more than what I can recognize on paper, but this is a start for sure!

Now it is your turn to be grateful and acknowledge the things in your life. Make a list of ten things you are grateful for. Each day for the next ten days add ten items to your list. By day ten, you should have over a hundred things you are grateful for! Just look at the list you will create. Will it get tough to create the list? Absolutely! But that's the challenge. You get to dig and dive deep into your life and find all the small things you are grateful for! This list is all about you!

But why? Why should you make this list and add to it daily? Why should you even be grateful? Simple. When we acknowledge the things we have, that shows the universe that we appreciate it. It allows for the universe (or your higher power) to bless you with more! It goes back to childhood when parents would say, "When you start appreciating what you have then you could have more." The Same thing goes for the journey in life. Appreciate what you have girlfriend so that the universe can add to it! The daily list is just to get the ball rolling and show yourself things you are grateful for! Allow it to flow. Try to make your list a part of your morning routine. Show yourself what you have accomplished! Be grateful for all of your experiences, including those you felt were negative.

Here is a start to your list:

DAY 1: Today I am grateful for

Once you complete your list every day, read it out loud. Read it to a close friend and have them do it with you! Show yourself and someone the things you are grateful for! Hell, if you want a challenge, get everyone at work or school and create a big list of all that you are thankful for. You are a worthy woman, and worthy women have gratitude!

Saying No Is A Yes For You And Them

N ow, ladies, I know you have been in a situation where you really really really wanted to say no, but you didn't for whatever reason. How did you feel after saying yes when you really wanted to say no. I could only imagine the pressure and uneasy feeling of doing something opposite of what you wanted to. Take it from me, or just that uncomfortable experience and stand in truth. When you say no to someone, it is not a negative thing. It allows growth for you and them. For you, saying no allows you to be honest with someone on the feedback you are giving them. It allows you to show them you really care because you are responding to how they are showing up. For them, it allows honest feedback. If they are asking you a yes or no question and you answer with a no, it shows them improvements or adjustments may be needed. Feedback is a great tool when we use it positively. But none the less it is feedback. It allows us to receive the message of what we are putting out in the world. If we aren't given honest feedback, we probably wouldn't be able to see how we are showing up.

We will look at some examples of what saying no can do. The examples are from people who consistently ask you for the same things.

Mom, can I have money?'

Saying no allows your child to come up with creative ideas to increase their own financial wealth.

Sis, can I use the car?

Saying no allows them to create transportation in their life.

Hey, can you watch the kids tonight?

Saying no allows you to value your time and energy. This can create a dialogue between you and that individual so they can ask in advance and not the day of.

Whatever the question may be there is a win-win for you and for them. So I challenge you to write down a list of ten people who consistently ask for something from you. Recalling the experiences of being annoyed by the person or frustrated with them may bring back old feelings, and that's okay. Write their name down and everything they ask you for. THEN come up with two possible responses that allow a win for you and a win for them. Saying no is a neutral place just like saying yes. We can create experiences from a yes and from a no.

Let them create their own experiences, but you get to stand in your power and allow a NO to exist for yourself.

—⁓⁓—

Neutral

I n science, we're taught that a neutron is neutral because it doesn't have a negative or positive charge. A battery has a positive and a negative end. Water can be hot or cold. The weather outside could be freezing or scorching. You can be up or down. Happy or sad. Black or white. Do you see what I'm doing here? Everything can be something or something else, but there is a balance to it all!

Now apply that to life. When a situation arises who determines if it is positive or negative? You do. Who has the final say so if something is going to affect you significantly or in a small amount? You do. Who can change anything from a negative to a positive? You Do. You are absolutely right! You have the ability, energy, and brains to make anything in your life a negative or positive. Now I'm not saying life is easy because we all know life will happen and things will happen that are out of our control. And of course, you can't control the universe and every single detail of your journey. If you could, you probably wouldn't have experienced as much as you already have. You wouldn't have problems, and you would probably be the richest person in the world, living on an island, with no stress. Lol.

But you have the ability to shift your energy and allow things to serve you and be positive for you. There is a reason for all things, and we get to allow ourselves to enjoy our personal journey. So when you hit your toe on the corner of the bed and want to swear to the world, take a step back, slow down, and be conscious of what you are doing. Maybe the universe was purposely slowing you down, but that pain you feel is the example of something that could have been negative.

A broken bone or limb, a death in the family, birth, a car wreck, receiving a bonus, a new job, promotion, and a jackpot winning are all examples of things that can happen in life. Which events are positive? Which events are negative? Most will say winning a jackpot, giving birth, being promoted, new job, and a bonus is positive while a broken bone or limb, a death in the family, and a car wreck are all negatives. Again, use this example and see who made them negative or positive. YOU DID. No one else! If you take away personal experience and just look at the event as a neutral event, you then have the power of choice. You can choose if you will receive the event as a negative or positive. You allow yourself to control what happens next with those events and anything else that would happen in your life. The difference between receiving something as negative or positive and just allowing yourself to remain neutral is that you have the power of choice! You control the outcome of yourself and your journey. For most of us reading, this could be one of the hardest things for us to do. Everything we do in life is a practice. You get to practice remaining neutral in all things. This could be hard because the majority of your life you have already practiced being negative or positive towards most events. Say you lost your parent or siblings today. How would you feel? Hurt? Crushed? All of those emotions are great because that's what is coming up for you. You are human, and you get to feel. But remaining neutral in an event like this allows you to see how beautiful life was for that person. How they have blessed so many others. How they have taught you so much, and embracing the quality time that was spent between you. If you were to choose to be negative, you would miss out on all the beautiful things that happen in life and become depressed, angry, or even aggressive. Death can be a hard thing for many to swallow but if we switch the story we created about death to a positive one, it allows us to appreciate all that life was giving.

We can take any situation and remain neutral and turn it into a positive. Breakups, divorces, abuse, rape, etc. I include rape because I have been violated and since experiencing that event in my life and sharing the story I now want to inspire women and youth to heal their lives by sharing their stories and turn their pain into passion. It is not an overnight fix, but now I'm able to remain neutral and allow myself to control my responses to situations.

I want to remind you that this is simply a tool to practice. Not a quick overnight fix. Remaining neutral for any situation simply means when something comes up instead of reacting, take a step back, think, and choose the action that supports you in moving forward. Allowing yourself to remain in a neutral state lets you have control of the situation and not the situation over you.

The Little Girl Is Still There (Childhood)

I am a little princess in a castle with Prince charming. I have my mother who is the queen and my father who is the king. I have helpers who take care of me, and I eat whatever I want. I attend royal balls with fancy gowns, beautiful people, and decorations that would amaze the world. My castle is glorious, and I stay in the east quarter of the castle. I have tea time and go horseback riding daily. I am a princess, and this is who I'm meant to be.

What were the fun and exciting times when you were little? Were you daddy's little girl? The favorite granddaughter? The most loved girl in elementary? What was your story and where did she go? The little girl who loved life and had a care for everyone in the world?

We always can look at Cinderella and imagine us being in the fairy tale. Or look at any Disney princess and wishing it was us with the happily ever after, but do you realize we allowed life to destroy that happily ever after when we were little? When that one bad thing happens to us, we held on to it for a long time because as children we didn't have the tools to heal our hearts from heartbreaks. As you continued to grow up, suppressing that hurt, you became bitter. You allowed that pain to shape you into someone that always has to fight or to defend themselves.

But why? Why can't you be a princess all your life and when you hit adulthood transform into a Queen. You were meant to be one anyway. Do you even know who the little girl inside is anymore? Have you lost contact with her? Do you even dream anymore?

Ladies. You get to reconnect with the inner girl, the inner princess. You get to go back to when you were four or five years old and bring her back with you. Why? Because that girl is waiting on you, and never asked to be locked away. She is you and wants all her dreams to come true. When you live and enjoy your life, you are that little girl again.

If you have a daughter or niece how would you want her to feel in life? I'm sure you would at least want her to be happy and live how she would want to. Ding ding ding. Why can't you live how you would want them to? But you can. Every woman should feel like a queen in this world, and that can only happen with you! You get to allow yourself to be free. Become that unicorn and allow yourself to shine and be bright. Being different and unique is okay. That is what the world needs to see more of not less! Stop hiding your awesomeness because you are afraid to offend people or be too much. Girl, be all that you are and more! That little girl who had not one ounce of fear and lived life - become her again. Explore the possibilities. She is waiting for you to return so you all can be great together.

What does a queen consist of? For starters, unconditional love, strength, power, unity, ambition, eagerness, forgiveness, and will power. Mother Theresa was a queen. Oprah is a queen. Maya Angelou was a queen. Janet Jackson is a queen. Michelle Obama is a queen. And damn it. Your name gets to be right next to theirs as well because YOU ARE A QUEEN. No queen rules the same way, and that is great, but you get to start now. A Queendom is what you are creating in your life from here on out! You get to explore, live, vibrate, share, encourage, experience, and forgive! It's time to let all the things that hurt you go and start living life again.

So there is no exercise or homework because you get to discover on your own your inner child and allow that princess to come out!

Your Journey Of Empowering Women Starts Now!

Y ou have made it to the end, and you are in a place better than when you started. To forward this #MovementOfLove focus on and support others. You are a #WorthyWoman, and you get to unite and create other Worthy Women.

When we live our truth and support others to live in theirs, we co-create greatness together. When we allow ourselves to be in service and give back, we enable the blessing to be given. When we stop holding on to the past and vibrate higher, we allow growth and success. You're meant for greatness and as cliché as it may sound you are the only person standing you in your way.

So this journey that we have taken together has been beautiful, but it's time to lead your tribe on their journey. Worthy women create worthy leaders! This tribe is for all women.

My only request is to support the woman you may encounter to your left and to your right because no bond is stronger than when women come together and move forward together.

I can't wait to see your #WorthyWoman journey throughout the world and the things you create! If you only take away one thing from this entire book:

KNOW THAT YOU MATTER! YOU ARE PURPOSE! YOU ARE A QUEEN! YOU ARE A #WORTHYWOMAN, and YOU CAN HAVE IT ALL.

LOVE YOU QUEEN

YOU ARE A GODDESS! SO NEVER DIM YOUR LIGHT!

—∿—

About the Author

J oshua Phillips was born and raised in Houston, Texas. This empowered warrior and wholeness guide has sought to impact and guide individuals towards personal breakthroughs that wake them to become self-aware.

After a short career in customer service, modeling, aviation, military, and politics, Joshua has proven his knowledge and his natural instinct of understanding how to develop, train, and motivate individuals. Being raised by a single mother and later his grandmother, his extraordinary past has helped him understand and create positive content in support of women and youth; he sincerely and wholeheartedly believes his work will inspire a massive shift of transforming individuals towards self-empowerment and love.

His passion for opening individual's hearts, minds, and spreading positive energy has paved the way for him to enter the realm of coaching, especially for women and youth. He has coached clients on business development, relationships, and self-improvement and goes the extra mile to ensure his client's dreams and aspirations become a reality.

He is on a mission to change the globe and instill love! He calls it a #MovementOFLove! His passion is to leave any individual filled with amazing tools so they can take on life as leaders, action-doers, and achievers.

When you are true to yourself, to your purpose and passion, and true to commitment, he believes we all can change the universe. Follow your heart while working with him and practice his principals, anything is always possible!

SO NOW WHAT? Let's run into battle and kick life's ass together! Contact me at iiamjoshuaphillips@gmail.com.

Printed in the United States
By Bookmasters